Pushing The Rock
Understanding The Physical And Spiritual Concept Of Pushing The Rock

---

Sandra B. Randolph

Published by: LifeSkill® Institute, Inc.   SAN: 255-8440
Copyright © 2018 by Sandra B. Randolph

All rights reserved. No part of this book may be used, reproduced or transmitted in any form or by any means, electronic or mechanical, including photocopying and recording, or by any information storage or retrieval system, without written permission from the publisher, except by a reviewer who wishes to quote brief excerpts in connection with a group study, review in a newspaper, magazine, or electronic publication. Requests for permission should be addressed in writing to:
Sandra B. Randolph, P.O. Box 847 Wilmington, NC 28402

Library of Congress Cataloging-in-Publication Data

Randolph, Sandra B. 1955—
Pushing the Rock by Sandra B. Randolph

ISBN 978-1-890199-06-7   paperback edition
ISBN 978-1-890199-07-4   hardcover edition

Library of Congress Control Number:
1. Religion I. Title   II. Randolph, Sandra B.
2. Self-Help/Self-Improvement
3. Wellness
4. Christian Life
5. Spiritual Growth

Printed in the United States of America

Publisher:
Lifeskill Institute Inc. SAN: 255-8440
P.O. Box 302
Wilmington, NC 28402
(800) 570-4009

Email: srandolph801@hotmail.com

Dedication

I dedicate this book to my friend, Dr. Michael Graybar of Graybar Chiropractic and Rehab, Pastor Brad Carter, Pastor of Kingdom Builders, to all Christians and non-Christians who will go through an unexpected trial, tribulation or personal sickness. I pray that this book encourages you to remain strong. I pray that you will find strength, comfort and hope as you read our story. I pray you will understand the physical and spiritual concept of Pushing the Rock.

Pushing The Rock

Contents

Introduction 7

Pushing The Rock 9

Routine Check-Up/The Process 13

Meeting With The Heart Doctor 15

Stress Test 17

Wedding Anniversary 19

Another EKG Done 21

Women's Retreat 23

Remembering God's Promises 25

Catherization Done 27

Faith Tried/Pushing the Rock 31

Meeting the Surgeon / Surgery Scheduled 33

Last Public Sermon 37

First Symptoms Experienced 39

Admitted To NHRMC 41

Support System 45

Pushing The Rock

The Surgery 47

Recovery Time 49

The Heart Converted 51

The Healing Process 55

Discharged From The Hospital 57

Readjusting At home 59

Follow Up Visits And Discharge Orders 61

First Sermon To The Public After Recovery 63

Pushing The Rock 65

Conclusion 67

Be Encouraged by William Becton

About the Author 69

Pictures of our Story 71

Introduction

This is the story about my husband, whose name is Ricky Henry Randolph.

This is my version of what happened when our world turned upside down.

This man loves the Lord with all his might. He pastors Uplifting Faith Ministries, Inc., located at 1020 Princess Street in Wilmington, North Carolina, along with myself, Sandra Randolph. We have four sons and thirteen grandchildren.

We also have several churches under our leadership, which we operate in the office of Apostles, and it can be stressful.

This man is a teacher from the heart. His daily routine includes morning devotion, going to Planet Fitness five days a week, working out a minimum of one hour and a half per day. He teaches piano lessons, not only in Wil-

Pushing The Rock

mington, NC, but also in Bolivia, NC, on Tuesdays. He also goes to Elderhaus PACE at Canterbury, which is an adult Day Care Center which presents an alternative to nursing home care and ministers to the elderly on Tuesdays as well. Wednesdays are spent at Uplifting Faith Ministries, Inc. teaching Bible study at 12:00 noon and again at 7:00 p.m., also on Wednesdays at 6:00 p.m. we minister at Cypress Pointe Rehabilitation and Nursing Facility. Sunday mornings, there are Praise Team rehearsals, Sunday School, morning worship and ministering to the needs of the people. Mondays are his days off from his paying job, but he has chores at home, to help me out.

Proverbs 3:5-6 – Trust in the Lord with all thine heart; and lean not unto thine own understanding. In all thy ways acknowledge him, and he shall direct thy paths.

Pushing the Rock

The cover of this book has a huge rock on it, which is where the title of this book came from. I was at Dr. Michael Graybar's office one Monday and was upset over all that my husband and I were going through. His words of encouragement were, "Oh, he is pushing the rock." He said, "You never heard the story about pushing the rock?" "No," I said, "Tell me." He said, "Wait a minute, let me call my pastor and let him tell you, because I am going to mess it up."

After my treatment was done, he called his pastor. I was on the phone with someone who did not know me personally, but recognized me by my spirit. Pastor Carter proceeded to tell me the following story. He said, "There was a young boy who had a dream. In that dream he saw a huge rock that was placed in his front yard and his instructions from God was to push the rock

Pushing The Rock

daily.

The young boy woke up and realized that he was dreaming, but when he looked outside, there was this huge rock in his yard. The Lord's instruction was, to push the rock. The boy was obedient. Every day, all during the day, he would push the rock. All the neighbors started laughing at him because he was pushing a rock that was not going anywhere. This happened to him during the summer while he was out of school.

After returning to school, his classmates were all laughing at him about pushing a rock that was not moving. Walking home from school, he had a talk with God, telling Him how he was tired of pushing the rock and people were making fun of him. God's response was, "Push the rock."

The next day walking home from school, he noticed a car had flipped over in the river. He was able to get to the car and found a man and his daughter were trapped inside and would drown if he didn't do something. The Lord told him to go and lift the bumper of the car and he could help get them out. Immediately, they were able to get out safely and he became an instant hero in the town. While he was pushing the rock, as instructed, he was building muscles.

The young boy went home all hyped up and thanked God for allowing him to save the man and his daughter. God spoke and told him because of his obedience of pushing the rock, as instructed, he was able to save the man and his daughter."

I was in tears by this part of the story, and Pastor Carter encouraged me and told me that my husband has been pushing the rock by going to the gym every day and was building his heart up for the surgery. He said, "I can't wait to hear the testimony of what God is

Pushing The Rock

going to do through your husband." I couldn't talk anymore because I walked out of Dr. Graybar's office in tears. I left there knowing without any doubt that God had my husband in His hands.

We had to literally eat those words daily.

Routine Check-up/The Process

June 2016 – Apostle Ricky Henry Randolph, went to his medical doctor for a routine physical exam. During his exam, his calcium level showed up as 2400 while normal levels are 400. This was a red flag for his medical doctor and he immediately sent him to a heart doctor.

Pushing The Rock

Meeting with the Heart Doctor

Normally, he would go to the doctor alone, but this was beginning to sound serious and I did not like what I was hearing. We are Christians and we can pray our way through this, was my thought. Wait a minute, I was not sending prayer. I felt like I needed to be with him to pray.

<u>James 5:14-16</u> – Is any sick among you? Let him call for the elders of the church; and let them pray over him, anointing him with oil in the name of the Lord: And the prayer of faith shall save the sick, and the Lord shall raise him up; and if he have committed sins, they shall be forgiven him. Confess your faults one to another, and pray one for another, that ye may be healed. The effectual fervent prayer of a righteous man availeth much.

Pushing The Rock

On July 11, 2016, we met with the heart doctor, Dr. Martin J. Conley. After reading the reports from my husband/s medical doctor, Dr. Conley had an EKG ordered and scheduled him for a stress test.

Stress Test

The stress test was scheduled for July 27, 2016, but I was unable to go with him. One of the members of our church, Deacon Joseph Jenkins volunteered to accompany him. God will put people in place to help you, if you accept their help. We were at the point of needing others to join us in prayer. Prayer requests were sent out to so many people. They were praying for my husband. We found out that there were many pastors that had already gone through the same procedure. They were certainly, asked to pray as well. Some even called to encourage us and told us if we needed anything, they were just a phone call away.

Pushing The Rock

Wedding Anniversary

August 12, 2016 was our 21st wedding anniversary. Of course, the enemy started playing with our minds. My thought pattern was, what if this is our last anniversary. What if.... what if.... what if... I had to really pray harder and began rebuking the enemy, in my mind. I had to remind God of His promises. We decreed healing in the name of Jesus. My husband had a history of heart disease in his family. His father died, from a heart attack when my husband was twelve years old. All these thoughts were running through my head. Lord what if...what if... Please help me. Yes, I am a believer, but my faith was wavering. The prayer warriors started praying for me as well. Prayer changes things. I needed that peace that surpasses all understanding. One of the ministries in our church, The Youth on the Move for Christ purchased me a peace lily. It was huge, and it is still growing. They knew how I cherished a peace lily and needed to be reminded of the peace of God that surpasses ALL of my understanding.

Phillippians 4:7 – And the peace of God, which passeth all understanding, shall keep your hearts and minds through Christ Jesus.

Another EKG Done

August 22, 2016, we had to go back to Dr. Conley's office (heart doctor) for another EKG. Dr. Conley called us in a side office where we looked at the computer and saw that the first EKG, the Stress Test and the second EKG all showed signs of abnormalities. Pandora was playing – "You Raise Me Up by Josh Groban." (When I am down and, oh my soul, so weary. When troubles come, and my heart burdened be. And I am still and wait here in the silence. Until you come and sit awhile with me. You raise me up, so I can stand on mountains. You raise me up, to walk on stormy seas. I am strong, when I am on your shoulders. You raise me up, to more than I can be. You raise me up, so I can stand on mountains. You raise me up to walk on stormy seas. I am strong when I am on your shoulders. You raise me up to more than I can be. You raise me up, so I can stand on mountains. You raise me up, to walk on stormy seas. I am strong, when I am on your shoulders. You raise me up, to more than I can be. You raise me up, so I can stand on mountains. You raise me up, to walk on stormy seas. I am strong, when I am on your shoulders. You raise me up to more than I can be. You raise me up to more than I can be.)

After hearing this, I knew that God had us. I told Dr. Conley we were in the right place. A few days later, Dr. Conley's nurse called to tell my husband that he could continue to go to the gym, but just walk on the treadmill or ride the bike, because he could actually have a heart attack at the gym. A spirit of fear was released. Immediately, we had to bind that spirit of fear and loose love, power and a sound mind according to:

II Timothy 1:7. – *For God hath not given us the spirit of fear; but of power, and of love, and of a sound mind.*

Women's Retreat

September 9, 2016 – Uplifting Faith Ministries, Inc. had their second women's retreat under the direction of Elder Carolyn J. Blue in Myrtle Beach, South Carolina. The Theme was "Don't Let Go." On the opening night, a prophetic word was given to my husband (which I knew would happen) stating that he is healed: "Don't let go, you are healed. You are healed on this side, saith the Lord."

Another word came forth, not just for him, but his wife as well. This was so profound because I had been diagnosed with thyroid disease and after surgery in 2001, I have to take meds daily to control it. Stress, and a lack of rest, has a tendency, to get my thyroid off track. During the whole process, my stress levels were very high, but I had no problems with my thyroid. God is a healer. The retreat was all that and then some. We

Pushing The Rock

returned home early Sunday morning in time for Sunday School. We were pumped up on the word. - "Don't Let Go!"

Remembering God's Promises

Isaiah 53:5 – *But he was wounded for our transgressions, he was bruised for our iniquities: the chastisement of our peace was upon him; and with his stripes we are healed.*

I Peter 2:24 – *Who his own self bare, our sins in his own body on the tree, that we, being dead to sins, should live unto righteousness: by whose stripes ye were healed.*

Between Isaiah 53 and I Peter 2 you is healed (not proper English).

We are standing on His promises.

Pushing The Rock

Catheterization Done

Monday, September 12, 2016 – 6:00 a.m. We arrived at NHRMC for the catheterization to be done on his heart. My husband was taken back in preparation for the catheterization. I was there alone in the intensive care waiting room, but I was not alone. I had my headphones in my ear and I kept listening to "I Believe," by James Fortune. All of a sudden, I could hear my husband telling me how cold he was. I had my blanket and just could not get warm. I was interceding for him and knew it. After being there in a waiting room, full of folk, feeling the presence of the Lord, tears falling down my cheeks, I looked around thinking, they must think I am crazy. I really did not care.

Deacon and Prophetess Hines came just as they called me to come back and talk to the doctor. I was not worried at all. Little did I know, that meeting would change the course of our lives for a while. The surgeon

Pushing The Rock

told me and my husband that he tried to do the catheterization, but there were three blocked arteries. Two arteries were blocked at 90% and one was at 65%. I could not believe what I was hearing. I asked him to please repeat what he just said. He did and told us that he could not unblock the arteries at that time because the hospital would bill us for ten thousand dollars ($10,000) because our insurance would not pay for the surgery, unless he had been taking two separate heart meds for a minimum of two weeks.

The attending physician wrote him a prescription for the second heart med for him to start taking immediately, and to go back to his heart doctor after taking it. I went back to the waiting room to tell Deacon and Prophetess what the doctor said. I actually, broke down, and began to cry. I kept saying over and over – he is healed, on this side. He is healed on this side. My God is not a liar. I tried to get myself together so we (Deacon Hines,

Prophetess and myself) could go back and be with my husband. You have to realize that my husband and I both are saved. We believe in spiritual gifts. We are the pastors of Uplifting Faith Ministries, Inc. located at 1020 Princess Street, Wilmington, North Carolina. We have a healing and deliverance ministry. We believe in the five- fold ministry "BUT," we are now standing in the need of "uh, uh, uh" a miracle. We didn't feel like praying for anyone. We needed prayer. We needed someone praying for us. My husband got dressed. We went and got his prescription filled. We then went to Denny's for breakfast. That was one of the things that we did after each one of his appointments to reward ourselves. We were just trying to get to that place of being normal. Where was it? Where do we go from here? How do we act? How do we not react? So many questions. So many decisions to make. So much to do in preparation for the journey ahead of us.

Pushing The Rock

Philippians 4:13 – I can do all things through Christ which strengthens me.

We ordered breakfast. We looked at each other and re-affirmed our love. I promised him right then and there that I would not leave him for as long as he had to be in the hospital. I told him I would go home to shower, but I would be right back. "I promise" those were my words. So many tried to get me to go home while he was in the Intensive Care Unit, but I promised my husband that I would not leave him. I kept my word.

Faith Tried/Pushing the Rock

October 3, 2016 – 10:30 a.m. we met with Dr. Conley again. His nurse called after our visit and said Dr. Conley did not want him to do any strenuous exercises. He could go to the gym but could not do any heavy lifting of weights, etc. He could walk on the treadmill. My husband was crushed. He always went to the gym Monday through Friday for at least an hour and a half, each day. A seed of fear was planted. This was his way of pushing the rock.

Matthew 17:20b – If ye have faith, as a grain of mustard seed, ye shall say unto this mountain, Remove hence to yonder place; and it shall remove; and nothing shall be impossible unto you.

Somewhere between June 2016 and October 2016, I told Dr. Michael Graybar about my husband. Dr. Graybar stated that he needed to push the rock. The cover has a

Pushing The Rock

picture of a rock and it is based on the story that Dr. Graybar and Pastor Carter told me about pushing the rock. I have told this story so many times from that day until today, to encourage someone else on this journey. While driving home from Dr. Graybar's office, between Kerr Avenue and Gordon Road, I saw this huge rock in someone's yard. There it is again. A reminder that God has this. Keep pushing the rock.

Meeting the Surgeon/Surgery Scheduled

October 4, 2016 – 10:00 a.m. – Today we met with Dr. Kelly Nagasawa, the heart surgeon. He sat down and told us step by step what would take place. His chest would be cut down the middle, his heart would be lifted up, and placed on a ventilator for 45 minutes so that he would be able to work on it better to do the by-pass surgery. After surgery, he would still be on the ventilator and, gradually, would be taken off, of the ventilator to breathe on his own. Based on the individual, it could take up to two days to come off, of the ventilator. He would also be placed in the Cardio Intensive Care unit for two days, then placed on the 9th floor of the hospital for 4-7 days. He told us he was getting married and would be out of the office for 2 weeks, but if anything happened before he got back, his partners could do the surgery. He said he would be back in the office on October 24, 2016. We then scheduled his

Pushing The Rock

surgery for Wednesday, November 2, 2016. His pre-testing would be done the week before surgery. My husband told him that he had been going to the gym five times a week, but Dr. Conley told him that he only wanted him to walk on the treadmill. Dr. Nagasawa told him that he wanted him back in the gym with the same routine. He wanted him to continue pushing the rock as Dr. Graybar had said. He said he wanted to operate on a strong heart. Going back to the gym would help with that process.

My husband did go back to the gym, but the spirit of fear had been planted. We had to bind it, in the name of Jesus, and we released power, love and a sound mind, but he just could not get back to that hour and a half workout pattern.

Galatians 6:7-9 – Be not deceived: God is not mocked: for whatsoever a man soweth, that shall he also reap. For he that soweth to his flesh shall of the flesh reap corruption; but he that soweth to the Spirit shall of the Spirit reap life everlasting. And let us not be weary in well doing: for in due season we shall reap, if we faint not.

Pushing The Rock

Last Public Sermon

Sunday, October 16, 2016 – 4:00 p.m. My husband preached his last sermon for a while at the appreciation service for Dr. Mary C. Nixon at St. Phillips A.M.E. Zion Church, in Wrightsboro, NC. His topic was "Leave Me Alone, I Got Work to Do." It was a powerful prophetic sermon to Dr. Nixon, but he was also ministering to himself as well. Many came to the altar for prayer and were healed of their infirmities. Our leaders helped with the altar work. It is awesome when there is team work when it comes to praying for people. We trained our leaders to help in the work of the kingdom. Our motto is, "The more you do, the less we have to do." We don't have time to be jealous of our leaders or their gifts. We all work together.

We made it home afterwards, exhausted. Still not fully understanding what was ahead for us, we just knew that we had to trust God.

Pushing The Rock

<u>*Proverbs 3:5-6 states*</u> *– Trust in the Lord with all thine heart; and lean not unto thine own understanding. In all thy ways acknowledge him, and he shall direct thy paths. We had to eat this scripture daily.*

First Symptoms Experienced

<u>Saturday, October 22, 2016 – 7:00 a.m.</u> He went at his normal time to go and get the bread for the bread ministry that we have at UFM. It was not until then, that be began to experience some discomfort in his chest. Being the type of person that he is, he thought it would get better. By the time he got back to the church and had a cup of decaf coffee, the pain eased up. I arrived at the church around 1:00 p.m. to put the chairs back after the carpet had been shampooed. He was finishing his last piano lesson when I got there. At the end of the lesson, he told me he was going to go to Medac because he was experiencing some discomfort in his chest. My reply was, "If you don't get your behind in my car, you better." Straight to NHRMC emergency room we went. I informed the staff at the ER that he was scheduled to have a triple by-pass on November 2, 2016, but he was having chest pains now. They imme-

Pushing The Rock

diately took him in the back. An EKG was done, and blood work taken. For precautions, they decided to keep him for observations.

Admitted to the Hospital

He was admitted to the 9th floor of New Hanover Regional Medical Center (heart floor – room 901). Early Sunday morning Dr. Nagasawa's partner came in saying he would take my husband down for the triple by-pass surgery, Sunday evening. He seemed very pushy and we were not feeling him. My husband said, "No. I got all of those tests that have to be done first," and he pointed to the board. Actually, the tests on the board were his pre-opt tests that he was supposed to have done for the original November 2nd scheduled surgery. The hospital had already started doing the test that were ordered when he was admitted. Dr. Nagasawa's partner saw our hesitation and backed off. I told him that Dr. Nagasawa would be back on the 24th, which was the next day.

Monday, October 24th – Dr. Nagasawa came to the hospital. He asked us what was going on? My husband told him, his side of the story. Dr. Nagasawa was ready

Pushing The Rock

for him to go home and come back the following Wednesday, but then he looked at me. I told him that my husband has his problems at night. He calls it heartburn. Dr. Nagasawa then said, "Ok. I have clinicals on Tuesday and usually finish up by 3:00 p.m., but I notice that my staff is tired by then." I informed him that we needed everyone to be rested. His surgery was then scheduled for Wednesday, October 26th at 7:30 a.m. The staff would take him down to the operating room by 5:00 a.m. since he was already a patient. All of his family and church family were informed of the surgery changes. The night before, the nurse gave him a sedative to help him rest because he was very anxious.

Wednesday, October 26th – My day started around 4:00 a.m. I got up, took a shower to get out of everyone's way. I got dressed, all but my shoes. I didn't cut any lights on in the room and finished getting dressed in the dark. My shoes felt funny. I went back in the bathroom and discovered that my shoes were on the wrong feet. I had to laugh at myself. I felt the Lord was telling me to get out of His way and trust Him. He was saying your shoes are on the wrong feet because you have to trust Me. At this time, I felt Him carrying us and a peace came over me.

Proverbs 3: 5 – Trust in the Lord with all thine heart; and lean not unto thine own understanding.

Pushing The Rock

Support System

By 5:00 a.m., my husband's room was full of supporters. The staff started coming in as well. We all prayed, and his nurse came in and prepared him for surgery (washed him with a special soap and he was shaved). Dr. Nagasawa came in and asked my husband if he was nervous. My husband said, "Yes." I asked Dr. Nagasawa if he was nervous. He said, "No." I said, "Ok, let's do this." I took his hand and whispered a brief prayer.

All of us to include – Elder Blue, my brother Wayne, Dr. Emerson, AJ, Kwabena (Baby Girl), Prophetess, Harold, Teresea and Cathy headed to the Surgical Pavilion. Others met us there – Jocelyn, Papa Joe, Greg, Loretta, Fred, Dr. Nixon and others.

Pushing The Rock

The Surgery

I really didn't know what to do from that moment onward. Dr. Nagasawa gave me a timeline to follow. By 9:30 a.m. someone should come and talk to us. It wasn't until 9:45 a.m. when the nurse reported that all was going well. She told us that my husband should be in intensive care by 10:30 a.m. At 10:45 a.m. they came to get us, informing me that only four could go with me. I told them immediate family (Greenville family) only please.

Seeing him on the ventilator was very hard. I talked to him and told him how good he looked. I actually, lied, but I was grateful that he made it through surgery. Now the healing could take place. We went back to the surgical pavilion to inform the others of the results. We thanked everyone for being there and asked for continued prayers. I also informed everyone that I was not allowing anyone to see him while in intensive care.

Pushing The Rock

My husband and I had already discussed that before surgery. We didn't want anyone seeing him like that. Pastor Stephen Bradley told us to keep the company at a minimum. He had also experienced heart surgery and knew first hand that too much company would hinder the recovery process. We took his advice.

Recovery Time

He was transferred to the Intensive Care Unit with visitation allowed only four times per day. I stayed at the hospital, leaving only to go home and take a shower and then returning, because I promised my husband that I would be there until he came home.

The second time that they allowed us to see him, he was awake. Remember, they told us it would probably take a couple of days for him to wake up. My God is so awesome. He woke up ahead of time. As a matter of fact, he did everything ahead of time.

Our third visit to the Intensive Care Unit the staff had him up walking. Yes, walking. My husband had been pushing the rock at the gym, with his daily routine, therefore he was giving that nurse a run for her money. She could hardly keep up with him because he was walking so fast.

Our cousin Cathy stayed with me the first night in the

Pushing The Rock

waiting room of the Intensive Care Unit. We pulled some hard chairs together and slept downstairs. The nurse told me if I couldn't sleep, she would let me come and see him. When I went to see him, they had a mask over his face. I was a little upset because I didn't expect to see that. When I asked why they had the mask over his face, I was told he was not breathing 100% yet and the mask was helping him to breathe. I went back downstairs with Cathy and just prayed. Praying and reminding God of his promises.

Isaiah 53:5 – *But he was wounded for our transgressions, he was bruised for our iniquities: the chastisement of our peace was upon him; and with his stripes we are healed.*

I Peter 2:24 – *Who his own self bare, our sins in his own body on the tree, that we, being dead to sins, should live unto righteousness: by whose stripes ye were healed.*

The Heart Converted

After two days in Intensive Care he was transferred back to the 9th floor of the hospital. After a couple of days on the 9th floor, his nurse was concerned that his blood pressure and heart rate were irregular. In order to get the heart rate to beat at a regular pace, a Cardizem drip was ordered. This drip was supposed to lower his blood pressure, which would allow his heart rate to get into a regular rhythm. The Cardizem was administered for 6-8 hours. After the completion of the Cardizem drip, my husband was allowed to take a shower. He had to sit in a chair to shower. His family, BK, Lisa, Greg and Loretta went downstairs to get something to eat. While they were gone, his heart converted (the drug Cardizem worked and the heart went back to the regular sinus rhythm, which was a normal steady heart beat) and he passed out. The aide was in the shower with him and screamed at me to press the call bell on the bed. I

Pushing The Rock

pressed the call bell and ran out in the hallway calling for his nurse. Within 10 seconds, his room had about 10 staff members in it. He was still hooked up to the heart monitor and the staff there also saw what was going on. I found myself confused. I called Elder Blue and screamed, "PRAY NOW".I looked in my phone for BK's name and number who was downstairs. First of all, I could not remember my brother in law's name or anybody else's name. I began to pray and say, "Lord, please help me." Immediately, I found BK's number in my phone. He answered, and I screamed, "Come back NOW." By this time, I am shaking. The staff was amazing. Somebody took me out of the room to calm me down. In the hallway I saw BK, Lisa, Greg and Loretta. I fell on Loretta's shoulder and began to cry. Lisa is a medical doctor whose practice is in Tennessee. She was able to talk to the nurse, then came back and told me in layman's terms what actually happened. My husband's heart did a conversion. She said this is normal. The drug Cardizem worked. Normally when a person is on this drug, the conversion takes place while the patient is in the bed. Well, you guessed it, from that point, I did not leave his bedside. Visitation was then cancelled for anyone to see him. He needed to rest. He kept telling me over and over again, "Honey, I am ok, I am ok." Our son, Stretch, came to see him. He looked at me and told me how tired I looked and told me I needed to go home. I told him I would be ok because I promised my husband that I would not leave him, and I had to keep my word.

Pushing The Rock

The Healing Process

My husband's healing was a process that he had to go through. I am reminded of a butterfly, who is a caterpillar first. A caterpillar goes through four stages before becoming a butterfly. First the egg, larva (the caterpillar stage), pupa (the chrysalis phase) and adult. When it is ready, the caterpillar will find a suitable place and attach itself to a leaf with a sticky substance. This substance hardens to become the chrysalis (similar to a cocoon). The caterpillar sheds its exoskeleton for the last time. After 1-2 weeks, a butterfly emerges from the chrysalis. The butterfly has to push the rock, by breaking out of the cocoon. No one can help it break the cocoon. As the butterfly is pushing the shell of the cocoon (pushing the rock) his wings are strengthen.

In our daily lives, we as Christians don't want to go through anything. We want everything on a silver platter.

Pushing The Rock

II Timothy 2:11-13 – It is a faithful saying: For if we be dead with him, we shall also live with him: If we suffer, we shall also reign with him: if we deny him, he also will deny us: If we believe not, yet he abideth faithful: he cannot deny himself.

Discharged from the Hospital

<u>Monday, October 31, 2016</u> He was discharged. Finally, we would be able to sleep in our own beds and get back to our normal life. Our discharge orders were, that he was not to be left alone for four weeks. He did not qualify to be placed in a Rehab Center because he was doing so well. When showering, someone had to watch him. He had to use six different wash cloths when washing. He could ride in a car, in the back seat only, with his heart pillow. Also, he was told to start walking daily.

Pushing The Rock

Readjusting at Home

First of all, my husband could not sleep in our bed. He tried to get me to sleep there, but my orders were, he was not to be left alone. We were just blessed with a very nice sectional from one of our members, Shana Bailey, which was an on time blessing. This was where we slept for the first several weeks after his discharge.

After two weeks of him being home I was getting stir crazy. Kenisha Jones informed me that she would come and sit with him if I wanted to go somewhere. I took her up on her offer. She came, and I went to Walmart in Porter's Neck. I felt like I had died and went to heaven. Walmart was amazing. There was a frozen food section, meat section, clothes, shoes, and the list goes on and on. I called my friend, Ann McNeil and told her I was in Walmart. I went down every isle. She laughed at me. I stayed in Walmart for two hours. Then, I felt guilty for leaving my husband so long with Kenisha and she was

Pushing The Rock

six months pregnant. Time just went by so fast. I tasted freedom. When I went back home, I apologized to Kenisha for staying so long. She said it was not a problem. Therefore, I called Elder Blue, UFM's church administrator and told her I needed a babysitter everyday for two hours. The members volunteered with no hesitation. Dr. Emerson, Papa Joe, Evangelist Hall, Prophetess Hines and Elder Blue just to name a few. Papa Joe was assigned to walk with my husband, because I didn't always feel like walking. He was doing really well. He just was not 100% yet. One day I took him with me for a ride. He was in the back seat of the van. When we came back home, I got out of the van and went in the house, automatically locking the door. While in the house for about five minutes, I noticed that my husband was not in the house. I went back outside. He was still sitting in the van, trying to figure out how to get out. I was grateful that it was not hot, and he was not in danger of dying in a hot van. Each day he got stronger.

Follow-up Visits and Discharge Orders

After four weeks of healing we went first to Dr. Nagasawa, the heart surgeon who released him, after getting a smile from me. We told him how grateful we were for him. He told me he had to watch me and my facial expressions, because I made him think he was doing something wrong. No sir, you were amazing. He told us to call him if we ever needed him.

Our next follow up visit was to Dr. Conley, the heart doctor. He also discharged my husband but made a follow-up visit for next year. He iInformed him that he could go back to the gym. He could go back to pushing the rock. He also told him to start out slow and gradually get back to his normal routine.

Pushing The Rock

First Sermon to the Public after Recovery

December 11, 2016 – My husband did his first sermon to the public at Uplifting Faith Ministries, Inc., after triple by-pass surgery. His subject was – "It's A Process." His scripture came from:

***Psalms 51:12** – Restore unto me the joy of thy salvation; and uphold me with thy free spirit.*

<u>Romans 12</u>: 1-2 – I BESEECH you therefore, brethren, by the mercies of God, that ye present your bodies a living sacrifice, holy, acceptable unto, God, which is your reasonable service. And be not conformed to this world: but be ye transformed by the renewing of your mind, that ye many prove what is that good, and acceptable, and perfect will of God.

Pushing The Rock

You ought to be doing better. Know who you are.

Point #1 – Know God's good will (II Timothy 2:15)

Point #2 – Walk in God's acceptable will (Galatians 5:15) and

Point #3 – Live in God's perfect will (I John 4:12)

It's A Process.

Pushing the Rock

All of us have pushed the rock in some shape or form. We are praying that this book encourages you to continue pushing the rock. Pushing the rock can be going to bible study, attending Sunday School, taking bible classes, attending a bible-believing, bible-teaching church, studying God's word daily, so when trials and tribulations come (pushing the rock) you will be strong enough to go through the storm. You won't panic in the midst of it.

Pushing The Rock

Conclusion

I want to close this by penning the words to this song by William Becton, simply entitled –

Be Encouraged.

(chorus)

Be encouraged no matter what's going on,

He'll make it alright,

But you gotta stay strong.

Be encouraged no matter what's going on,

He'll make it alright,

But you gotta stay strong.

(verse 1)

I know right now it's impossible to see,

But God is gonna work it out if you just believe.

Remember this one thing while you're going through,

If God delivered Daniel, He'll do the same for you.

Pushing The Rock

(verse 2)

Hold on, trouble don't last always,

These trials are just a test, just a test

Of your faith.

So stand strong and dry your weeping eyes,

'Cause joy comes in the morning, and everything

Is gonna be alright.

(vamp)

Be encouraged, be encouraged

But you gotta stay strong –

Be encouraged.

About the Author

Dr. Sandra Burns Randolph, is the daughter of the late Deacon Alfred and Deaconess Louise I. Burns, who was educated in the public schools of Brunswick County, North Carolina, and furthered her education by attending Fayetteville State University, Fayetteville, North Carolina, Miller-Motte Business College, Wilmington, North Carolina, Florida Theological College, Fayetteville, North Carolina (satellite campus), Bread of Life Institute, Whiteville, North Carolina and Wilmington, North Carolina. Dr. Randolph has a Doctorate in Divinity, Doctorate in Ministry and a Doctorate in Theology and currently is the Dean of School at the Bread of Life Institute, Wilmington, North Carolina campus.

Dr. Randolph is married to Dr. Ricky Henry Randolph. Together they serve as Apostles with five churches under their leadership, with Uplifting Faith

Pushing The Rock

Ministries, Inc. being the headquarters, located in Wilmington, North Carolina.

Together they have four sons and thirteen grandchildren. Dr. Randolph's motto is – "I want to leave a place better than I found it."

Pictures of Our Story

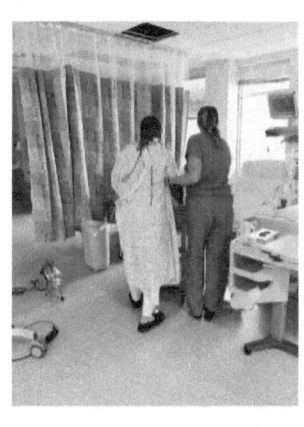
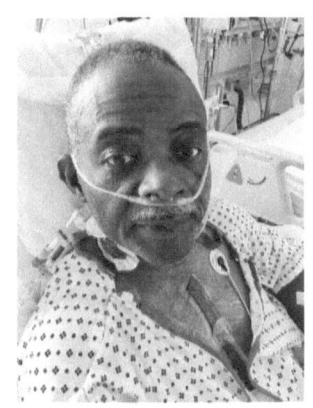
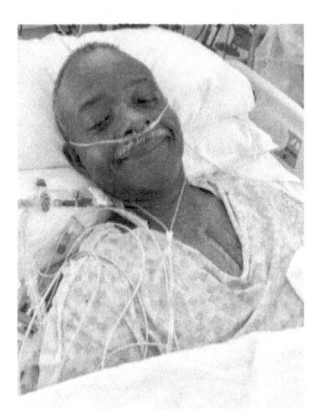
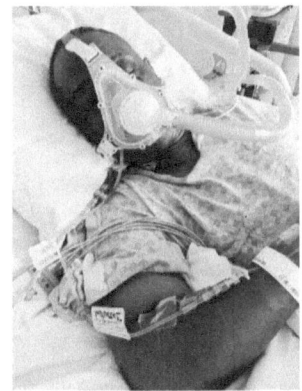

Pushing The Rock

Pictures of Our Story

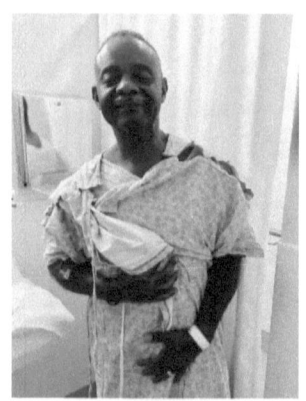
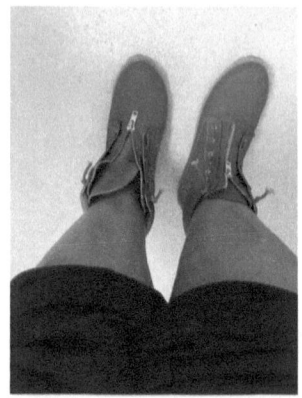
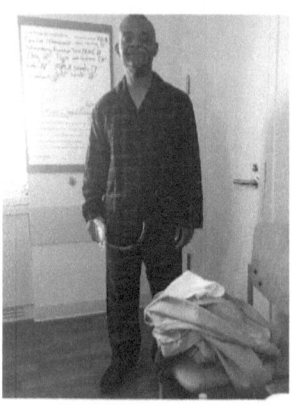
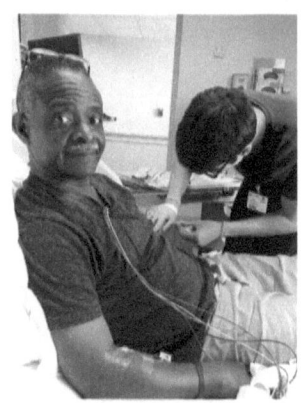
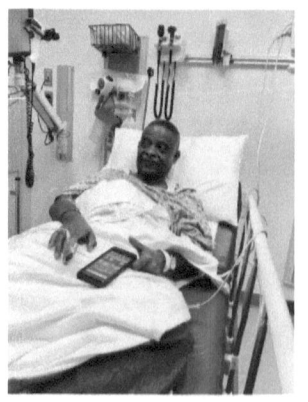

Pictures of Our Story

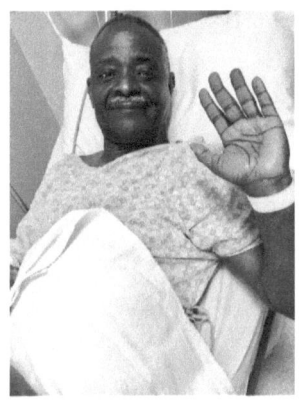 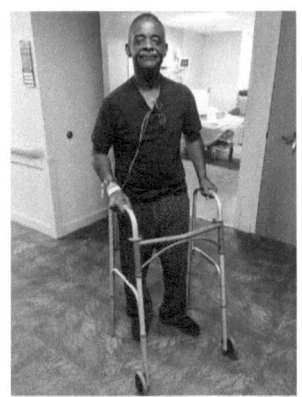

Pushing The Rock

Pushing The Rock

www.ingramcontent.com/pod-product-compliance
Lightning Source LLC
Chambersburg PA
CBHW021122080526
44587CB00010B/608